G000277501

JC

JOHN CLARE

Selected Poems

BLOOMSBURY
* POETRY *
CLASSICS

This selection by Ian Hamilton
first published 1996

Bloomsbury Publishing Plc, 2 Soho Square,
London W1V 6HB

A CIP catalogue record for this book
is available from the British Library

ISBN 0 7475 2917 5

Typeset in Great Britain by
Hewer Text Composition Services, Edinburgh
Printed in Great Britain by St Edmundsbury Press, Suffolk
Jacket design by Jeff Fisher

CONTENTS

A SCENE

The landscapes stretching view that opens wide
With dribbling brooks and rivers wider floods
And hills and vales and darksome lowering woods
With grains of varied hues and grasses pied
The low brown cottage in the shelter'd nook
The steeple peeping just above the trees
Whose dangling leaves keep rustling in the breeze
– And thoughtful shepherd bending oer his hook
And maidens stript haymaking too apear
And hodge a wistling at his fallow plough
And herdsman hallooing to intruding cow
All these with hundreds more far off and near
Approach my sight – and please to such excess
That Language fails the pleasure to express

THE HARVEST MORNING

Cocks wake the early morn wi' many a Crow
Loud ticking village clock has counted four
The labouring rustic hears his restless foe
And weary bones and pains complaining sore
Hobbles to fetch his horses from the moor
Some busy 'gin to team the loaded corn
Which night throng'd round the barns becrouded door
Such plentious scenes the farmers yards adorn
Such busy bustling toils now mark the harvest morn

The birdboy's pealing horn is loudly blow'd
The waggons jostle on wi' rattling sound
And hogs and geese now throng the dusty road
Grunting and gabbling in contension round
The barley ears that litter on the ground –
What printing traces mark the waggons way
What busy bustling wakens echo round
How drives the suns warm beams the mist away
How labour sweats and toils and dreads the sultry day

His scythe the mower oer his shoulder leans
And wetting jars wi' sharp and tinkling sound
Then sweeps again 'mong corn and crackling beans
And swath by swath flops lengthening oer the ground
While 'neath some friendly heap snug shelterd round
From spoiling sun lies hid their hearts delight
And hearty soaks oft hand the bottle round

Their toils pursuing with redoubl'd might
Refreshments cordial hail –
Great praise to him be due that brought thy birth to
  light

Upon the waggon now with eager bound
The lusty picker wirls the rustling sheaves
Or ponderous resting creaking fork aground
Boastful at once whole shocks o' barley heaves
The loading boy revengefull inly greaves
To find his unmatch'd strength and power decay
Tormenting horns his garments inter weaves
Smarting and sweating 'neath the sultry day
Wi' muttering curses stung he mauls the heaps away

A Motley group the Clearing field surounds
Sons of Humanity O neer deny
The humble gleaner entrance in your grounds
Winters sad cold and poverty is nigh
O grudge not providence her scant suply
You'll never miss it from your ample store –
Who gives denial harden'd hungry hound
May never blessings crow'd his hated door
But he shall never lack that giveth to the poor

Ah lovley Ema mingling wi' the rest
Thy beauties blooming in low life unseen
Thy rosey cheeks thy sweetly swelling breast
But ill it suits thee in the stubs to glean

O poverty! how basely you demean
The imprison'd worth your rigid fates confine
Not fancied charms of an arcadian queen
So sweet as Emas real beauties shine
Had fortune blest sweet girl this lot had neer been
  thine

The suns increasing heat now mounted high
Refreshment must recruit exausted power
The waggon stops the busy tools thrown bye
And 'neath a shock's enjoy'd the beavering hour
The bashful maid – sweet healths engaging flower
Lingering behind – oer rake still blushing bends
And when to take the horn fond swains implore
With feign'd excuses its dislike pretends
So pass the beavering hours – So harvest morning
  ends

O rural life what charms thy meaness hide
What sweet descriptions bards disdain to sing
What Loves what Graces on thy plains abide
O could I soar me on the muses wing
What riffel'd charms should my researches bring
Pleas'd would I wander where these charms reside
Of rural sports and beauties would I sing
Those beauties wealth which you but vain deride
Beauties of richest bloom superior to your pride

NOON

All how silent and how still,
Nothing heard but yonder mill;
While the dazzled eye surveys
All around a liquid blaze;
And amid the scorching gleams,
If we earnest look it seems
As if crooked bits of glass
Seem'd repeatedly to pass.
O! for a puffing breeze to blow,
But breezes all are strangers now.
Not a twig is seen to shake,
Nor the smallest bent to quake;
From the river's muddy side,
Not a curve is seen to glide;
And no longer on the stream,
Watching lies the silver bream,
Forcing from repeated springs,
'Verges in successive rings'.
Bees are faint and cease to hum,
Birds are overpow'r'd and dumb;
And no more love's oaten strains,
Sweetly through the air complains;
Rural voices all are mute;
Tuneless lies the pipe and flute;
Shepherds with their panting sheep,
In the swaliest corner creep;

And from the tormenting heat,
All are wishing to retreat;
Huddled up in grass and flow'rs,
Mowers wait for cooler hours;
And the cow-boy seeks the sedge,
Ramping in the woodland hedge,
While his cattle o'er the vales,
Scamper with uplifted tails;
Others not so wild and mad,
That can better bear the gad,
Underneath the hedge-row lunge,
Or, if nigh, in waters plunge;
O to see how flow'rs are took!
How it grieves me when I look: –
Ragged-robbins once so pink
Now are turn'd as black as ink,
And their leaves being scorch'd so much
Even crumble at the touch.
Drowking lies the meadow-sweet
Flopping down beneath one's feet;
While to all the flow'rs that blow,
If in open air they grow,
Th'injurious deed alike is done
By the hot relentless sun.
E'en the dew is parched up
From the teazle's jointed cup. –
O poor birds where must ye fly,
Now your water-pots are dry?

If ye stay upon the heath
Ye'll be chok'd and clamm'd to death,
Therefore leave the shadeless goss,
Seek the spring-head lin'd with moss

There your little feet may stand,
Safely printing on the sand;
While in full possession, where
Purling eddies ripple clear,
You with ease and plenty blest,
Sip the coolest and the best;
Then away and wet your throats,
Cheer me with your warbling notes;
'Twill hot Noon the more revive:
While I wander to contrive
For myself a place as good,
In the middle of a wood;
There, aside some mossy bank,
Where the grass in bunches rank
Lift it's down on spindles high,
Shall be where I'll choose to lie;
Fearless of the things that creep,
There I'll think and there I'll sleep;
Caring not to stir at all,
Till the dew begins to fall.

WHAT IS LIFE?

And what is Life? An hour-glass on the run
A mist retreating from the morning sun
  A busy bustling still repeated dream
Its length? A moment's pause, a moment's
  thought
  And happiness? A bubble on the stream
That in the act of siezing shrinks to nought

Vain hopes – what are they? Puffing gales of
  morn
That of its charms divests the dewy lawn
  And robs each flowret of its gem and dies
A cobweb hiding disappointments thorn
  Which stings more keenly thro' the thin
    disguise

And thou, O trouble? Nothing can suppose,
And sure the Power of Wisdom only knows,
  What need requireth thee.
So free and lib'ral as thy bounty flows,
  Some necessary cause must surely be.

And what is death? Is still the cause unfound
The dark mysterious name of horrid sound
  A long and ling'ring sleep the weary crave –
And peace – where can its happiness abound?
  No where at all but Heaven and the grave

Then what is Life? When stript of its disguise
   A thing to be desir'd it cannot be
Since every thing that meets our foolish eyes
   Gives proof sufficient of its vanity
'Tis but a trial all must undergo
   To teach unthankful mortals how to prize
That happiness vain man's denied to know
   Until he's call'd to claim it in the skies

TO MY COTTAGE

Thou lowly cot where first my breath I drew
Past joys endear thee childhoods past delight
Where each young summer pictures on my view
And dearer still the happy winter night
When the storm pelted down wi all his might
And roard and bellowd in the chimney top
And patterd vehement gainst the window light
And oer the threshold from the eaves did drop
How blest Ive listnd on my corner stool
Heard the storm rage and hugd my happy spot
While the fond parent wound her wirring spool
And spard a sigh for the poor wanderers lot
In thee sweet hut I all these joys did prove
And these endear thee wi eternal love

THE FATE OF GENIUS

Far from the life of market towns was seen
The humble hutts and spire of topal green
Were from the treetops that the hamlet shields
The white spire mounts and over looks the fields
Meeting the distant view of passing eyes
Were gentle memory often points and sighs
For there amidst the ignorance it wears
Wants chilling views and labours ceasless cares
A rustic genius from the darkness sprung
And sought the muses mid his toils and sung
And warmed with hopes while nature round him
smild
He humd their raptures and his fate beguild
But evil light thro his oblivion gleamd
The world wore smiles his artless hopes esteemd
And warmd with raptures better days to meet
They sought applause and realizd the cheat
Soon envys wasps around his sweets did swarm
And peacfull muses fled the rude alarm
Soon fames vain follys from their ambush rose
Friends while theyre powerless but in public foes
This praisd as fine what that as faults accusd
That urgd amendments which the next abusd
Thus mid the wild confusion babel raisd
By one advisd by others scofft and praisd
The damps of dissapointment provd too much
And warm hopes witherd at the chilly touch

Shrinking from life and hopes emblazoned noon
To witness envy had its own too soon
And what remains now linger to be blest
Aside that church were friendship tells the rest
Who placd a stone to mark his lowly sleep
That kindred hearts might find the spot to weep
Were the old sexton deaths undaunted slave
Who knew the bard and dug his early grave
To each request enquireys warmth may raise
Oft gives the tale of his unnoticd days
In hopes calm walks ere flattery smild his friend
And black injustice bade their journey end
'I knew him from a child' the clerk woud say
'And often noticd his dislike to play
Oft met him then lone left by woods and streams
Muttering about as people do in dreams
And neath lone bushes dropt about the field
Or peacfull hedges that woud shelter yield
With hand beneath his head in silence bent
Oft saw him sit and wonderd what it meant
Nor did his habits alter with his age
Still woods and fields his leisure did engage
Nor friends nor labour woud his thoughts beguile
Still dumb he seemd in company and toil
And if ones questions did his dreams supprise
His unconscern oft pausd in wrong replys

We wonderd many times as well we might
And doubted often if his mind was right
Een childern startld from his oddness ran
And shund his wanderings as "the crazy man"
Tho harmless as the things he mixd among
His ways was gentle and unknown to wrong
For ive oft markd his pity passing bye
Disturb the spiders web to save the flye
And saw him give to tyrant boys a fee
To buy the captive sparrows liberty
Each sundays leisure brought the woods their
  guest
And wildest spot which suited him the best
As bushy greens and valleys left untilld
Were weedy brooks went crooking as they willd
Were flags and reeds and sedge disorderd grew
These woud his abscence from his home pursue
And as he rambld in each peacfull round
Hed fancy friends in every thing he found
Muttering to cattle – aye and even flowers
As one in visions claimd his talk for hours
And hed oft wonder were we nought coud see
On blades of grass and leaves upon the tree
And pointed often in a wild supprise
To trifling hues of gadding butterflys
While if another made new marvels known
That seemd to me far wonderous then his own
Of ghosts hed seen that nightly walks decievd
He heeded not but laughd and disbelievd

Nights dismal tongues that hardest hearts affright
And all may hear that travel out at night
Her shadowd howling tenants fierce and grim
Tho trifles struck him – such was nought to him
At length twas known his ways by woods and
brooks
Were secret walks for making ryhmes and books
Which strangers bought and with amazment read
And calld him poet when they sought his shed
But men they said like serpents in the grass
That skulk in ways which learning has to pass
To slander worth which they woud feign posses
And dissapointment urges to suppress
Snarling at faults too bright for common minds
And hiding beautys wisdom warmly finds
Such marr'd his powers and slanderd in disguise
And tryd to black his merits with their lyes
And tho his friends the cheating fraud descryd
It hurt too earnest to be wipd aside
He dwindld down from too severe a blast
And hopes might wish to live that dyd as fast
Still he did live till real life seemd as gone
And his soul lingerd in a shadowd one
And yet he mingld in his favourd ways
And bar'd his forhead to the sunny days
Listning the lark on fountains moaning wave
As like a ghost as ever left its grave
And fled the world at last without a sigh
And dyd as gentle as a lamb woud dye

His learned friends said envys aim was blest
That malice killd him – they might know the best
Else folks less learnd to different causes led
Who read his books and marveld as they read
Were he so free of ghost and fairey talks
They thought he found them on his lonley walks
And that some secret which he faild to keep
Brought on their anger and his endless sleep
Be as it might his life fell in decay
And that stone tells when it was calld away
Were een the daiseys that around it spread
The gifts of spring to dress his lowly bed
Are often stole in garden scenes to grow
As relics of the dust that sleeps below
While the stones verses hid by summers weed
Which strangers eager trample down to read
Are bye the curious often written down
Tho they tell nought of praises or renown
"Here sleeps the hopes of one whose glowing birth
Was found too warm for this unfeeling earth
That frownd and witherd – yet the fruitfull stem
Hides here and buds with others warm as them
Waiting that sun that warms their bloom to smile
And welcome heaven as their native soil"'

TO THE RURAL MUSE

Simple enchantress, wreathd in summer blooms
Of slender bent stalks topt wi' feathery down
Heaths creeping fetch and glaring yellow brooms
And ash keys wavering on thy rushey crown
Simple enchantress how Ive wooed thy smiles
How often sought thee far from flusht renown
Sought thee unseen where fountain waters fell
Touchd thy wild reed unheard, in weary toils
And tho my heavy hand thy song defiles
Tis hard to leave thee and to bid farwell

Simple enchantress ah from all renown
Far far, my soul hath warmd in bliss to see
The varied figures on thy summer gown
That natures fingure works so witchingly
The silken leaf the varied colord flower
Green nestling bower bush and high towering
  tree
Brooks of the sunny green and shady dell
Ah sweet full many a time they've bin to me
And tho my weak song faulters sung to thee
I cannot wild enchantress bid farwell

Still feign to seek thee tho I wind the brook
When morning sunbeams oer the waters glide
And trace thy footsteps in the lonly nook
As evening moists the daisey by thy side
Ah if I wooe thee on thy bed of thyme
If courting thee be deemd ambitions pride
Ah tis so passing sweet wi thee to dwell
If love for thee in clowns be calld a crime
Forgive presumption – O thou queen of ryhme
Ive lovd thee long I cannot bid farwell

SONGS ETERNITY

What is songs eternity
Come and see
Can it noise and bustle be
Come and see
Praises sung or praises said
Can it be
Wait awhile and these are dead
Sigh sigh
Be they high or lowly bred
They die

What is songs eternity
Come and see
Melodys of earth and sky
Here they be
Songs once sung to adams ears
Can it be
– Ballads of six thousand years
Thrive thrive
Songs awakened with the spheres
Alive

Mighty songs that miss decay
What are they
Crowds and citys pass away
Like a day

Books are writ and books are read
What are they
Years will lay them with the dead
Sigh sigh
Trifles unto nothing wed
They die

Dreamers list the honey be[e]
Mark the tree
Where the blue cap tootle tee
Sings a glee
Sung to adam and to eve
Here they be
When floods covered every bough
Noahs ark
Heard that ballad singing now
Hark hark

Tootle tootle tootle tee
Can it be
Pride and fame must shadows be
Come and see
Every season own her own
Bird and be[e]
Sing creations music on
Natures glee
Is in every mood and tone
Eternity

The eternity of song
Liveth here
Natures universal tongue
Singeth here
Songs Ive heard and felt and seen
Everywhere
Songs like the grass are evergreen
The giver
Said live and be and they have been
For ever

From THE SHEPHERD'S CALENDAR

JUNE

Now summer is in flower and natures hum
Is never silent round her sultry bloom
Insects as small as dust are never done
Wi' glittering dance and reeling in the sun
And green wood fly and blossom haunting bee
Are never weary of their melody
Round field hedge now flowers in full glory twine
Large bindweed bells wild hop and streakd
  woodbine
That lift athirst their slender throated flowers
Agape for dew falls and for honey showers
These round each bush in sweet disorder run
And spread their wild hues to the sultry sun
Were its silk netting lace on twigs and leaves
The mottld spider at eves leisure weaves
That every morning meet the poets eye
Like faireys dew wet dresses hung to dry
The wheat swells into ear and leaves below
The may month wild flowers and their gaudy show
Bright carlock bluecap and corn poppy red
Which in such clouds of colors wid[e]ly spread
That at the sun rise might to fancys eye
Seem to reflect the many colord sky
And leverets seat and lark and partridge nest
It leaves a schoolboys height in snugger rest

And oer the weeders labour overgrows
Who now in merry groups each morning goes
To willow skirted meads wi fork and rake
The scented hay cocks in long rows to make
Were their old visitors in russet brown
The hay time butterflyes dance up and down
And gads that teaze like whasps the timid maid
And drive the herdboys cows to pond and shade
Who when his dogs assistance fails to stop
Is forcd his half made oaten pipes to drop
And start and halloo thro the dancing heat
To keep their gadding tumult from the wheat
Who in their rage will dangers overlook
And leap like hunters oer the pasture brook
Brushing thro blossomd beans in maddening haste
And stroying corn they scarce can stop to taste
Labour pursues its toil in weary mood
And feign woud rest wi shadows in the wood
The mowing gangs bend oer the beeded grass
Were oft the gipseys hungry journeying ass
Will turn its wishes from the meadow paths
Listning the rustle of the falling swaths
The ploughman sweats along the fallow vales
And down the suncrackt furrow slowly trails
Oft seeking when athirst the brooks supply
Were brushing eager the brinks bushes bye
For coolest water he oft brakes the rest
Of ring dove brooding oer its idle nest

And there as loath to leave the swaily place
He'll stand to breath and whipe his burning face
The shepherds idle hours are over now
Nor longer leaves him neath the hedgrow bough
On shadow pillowd banks and lolling stile
Wilds looses now their summer friends awhile
Shrill whistles barking dogs and chiding scold
Drive bleating sheep each morn from fallow fold
To wash pits were the willow shadows lean
Dashing them in their fold staind coats to clean
Then turnd on sunning sward to dry agen
They drove them homeward to the clipping pen
In hurdles pent were elm or sycamore
Shut our the sun - or in some threshing floor
There they wi scraps of songs and laugh and [t]ale
Lighten their anual toils while merry ale
Goes round and gladdens old mens hearts to praise
The thread bare customs of old farmers days
Who while the shrinking sheep wi trembling fears
Lies neath the snipping of his harmless sheers
Recalls full many a thing by bards unsung
And pride forgot - that reignd when he was young
How the hugh bowl was in the middle set
At breakfast time as clippers yearly met
Filld full of frumity were yearly swum
The streaking sugar and the spotting plumb
Which maids coud never to the table bring
Without one rising from the merry ring

To lend a hand who if twas taen amiss
Woud sell his kindness for a stolen kiss
The large stone pitcher in its homly trim
And clouded pint horn wi its copper rim
Oer which rude healths was drank in spirits high
From the best broach the cellar woud supply
While sung the ancient swains in homly ryhmes
Songs that were pictures of the good old times

From THE SHEPHERD'S CALENDAR

NOVEMBER

The village sleeps in mist from morn till noon
And if the sun wades thro tis wi a face
Beamless and pale and round as if the moon
When done the journey of its nightly race
Had found him sleeping and supplyd his place
For days the shepherds in the fields may be
Nor mark a patch of sky – blindfold they trace
The plains that seem wi out a bush or tree
Wistling aloud by guess to flocks they cannot see

The timid hare seems half its fears to loose
Crouching and sleeping neath its grassy lare
And scarcly startles tho the shepherd goes
Close by its home and dogs are barking there
The wild colt only turns around to stare
At passers bye then naps his hide again
And moody crows beside the road forbear
To flye tho pelted by the passing swain
Thus day seems turned to night and trys to
  wake in vain

The Owlet leaves her hiding place at noon
And flaps her grey wings in the doubting light
The hoarse jay screams to see her out so soon
And small birds chirp and startle with affright

Much doth it scare the superstitious wight
Who dreams of sorry luck and sore dismay
While cow boys think the day a dream of night
And oft grow fearful on their lonly way
Who fancy ghosts may wake and leave their
graves by day

The cleanly maiden thro the village streets
In pattens clicks down causways never drye
While eves above head drops – were oft she meets
The schoolboy leering on wi mischiefs eye
Trying to splash her as he hurrys bye
While swains afield returning to their ploughs
Their passing aid wi gentle speech apply
And much loves rapture thrills when she alows
Their help wi offerd hand to lead her oer the
sloughs

The hedger soakd wi the dull weather chops
On at his toils which scarcly keeps him warm
And every stroke he takes large swarms of drops
Patter about him like an april storm
The sticking dame wi cloak upon her arm
To guard against a storm walks the wet leas
Of willow groves or hedges round the farm
Picking up aught her splashy wanderings sees
Dead sticks the sudden winds have shook from off
the trees

The boy that scareth from the spirey wheat
The mellancholy crow – quakes while he weaves
Beneath the ivey tree a hut and seat
Of rustling flags and sedges tyd in sheaves
Or from nigh stubble shocks a shelter thieves
There he doth dithering sit or entertain
His leisure hours down hedges lost to leaves
While spying nests where he spring eggs hath taen
He wishes in his heart twas summer time again

From THE PROGRESS OF RHYME

O soul enchanting poesy
Thoust long been all the world with me
When poor thy presence grows my wealth
When sick thy visions gives me health
When sad thy sunny smile is joy
And was from een a tiney boy
When trouble was and toiling care
Seemed almost more then I could bear
While thrashing in the dusty barn
Or squashing in the ditch to earn
A pittance that would scarce alow
One joy to smooth my sweating brow
Where drop by drop would chase and fall
– Thy presence triumphed over all
The vulgar they might frown and sneer
Insult was mean – but never near
Twas poesys self that stopt the sigh
And malice met with no reply
So was it in my earlier day
When sheep to corn had strayed away
Or horses closen gaps had broke
Ere sunrise peeped or I awoke
My masters frown might force the tear
But poesy came to check and cheer
It glistened in my shamed eye
But ere it fell the swoof was bye

I thought of luck in future days
When even he might find a praise
I looked on poesy like a friend
To cheer me till my life should end
Twas like a parents first regard
And love when beautys voice was heard
Twas joy twas hope and may be fear
But still twas rapture every where
My heart were ice unmoved to dwell
Nor care for one I loved so well
Thro rough and smooth thro good and ill
That led me and attends me still
It was an early joy to me
That joy was love and poesy
And but for thee my idle lay
Had neer been urged in early day
The harp imagination strung
Had neer been dreamed of – but among
The flowers in summers fields of joy
Id lain an idle rustic boy
No hope to think of fear or care
And even love a stranger there
But poesy that vision flung
Around me as I hummed or sung
I glowered on beauty passing bye
Yet hardly turned my sheepish eye
I worshiped yet could hardly dare
To show I knew the goddess there

Lest my presumptious stare should gain
But frowns ill humour or disdain
My first ambition was its praise
My struggles aye in early days
Had I by vulgar boldness torn
That hope when it was newly born
By rudeness gibes and vulgar tongue
The curse of the unfeeling throng
Their scorn had frowned upon the lay
And hope and song had passed away
And I with nothing to attone
Had felt myself indeed alone
But promises of days to come
The very fields would seem to hum
Those burning days when I should dare
To sing aloud my worship there
When beautys self might turn its eye
Of praise – what could I do but try
Twas winter then – but summer shone
From heaven when I was all alone
And summer came and every weed
Of great or little had its meed
Without its leaves there wa'nt a bower
Nor one poor weed without its flower
Twas love and pleasure all along
I felt that Id a right to song
And sung – but in a timid strain
Of fondness for my native plain

For every thing I felt a love
The weeds below the birds above
And weeds that bloomed in summers hours
I thought they should be reckoned flowers
They made a garden free for all
And so I loved them great and small
And sung of some that pleased my eye
Nor could I pass the thistle bye
But paused and thought it could not be
A weed in natures poesy
No matter for protecting wall
No matter tho they chance to fall
Where sheep and cows and oxen lie
The kindly shower when theyre a dry
Falls upon them with cheering powers
As when it waters garden flowers
They look up with a blushing eye
Upon a tender watching sky
And still enjoy the kindling smile
Of sunshine tho they live with toil
As garden flowers with all their care
For natures love is even there
And so it cheered me while I lay
Among their beautiful array
To think that I in humble dress
Might have a right to happiness
And sing as well as greater men
And then I strung the lyre agen

And heartened up oer toil and fear
And lived with rapture every where
Till day shine to my themes did come
Just as a blossom bursts to bloom
And finds its self in thorny ways
So did my musings meet wi praise
And tho no garden care had I
My heart had love for poesy
A simple love a wild esteem
As heart felt as the linnets dream
That mutters in its sleep at night
Some notes from extacys delight
Thus did I dream oer joys and lye
Muttering dream songs of poesy
The storm was oer and hue and cry
With her false pictures herded bye
With tales of help where help was not
Of friends who urged to write or blot
Whose taste were such that mine were shame
Had they not helpt it into fame
Poh let the idle rumour ill
Their vanity is never still
My harp tho simple was my own
When I was in the fields alone
With none to help and none to hear
To bid me either hope or fear
The bird and bee its chords would sound
The air humed melodys around

I caught with eager ear the strain
And sung the music oer again
The Fields and woods are still as mine
Real teachers that are all divine
So if my song be weak or tame
Tis I not they who bear the blame
But hope and cheer thro good and ill
They are my aids to worship still
Still growing on a gentle tide
Nor foes could mar or friends could guide
Like pasture brooks thro sun and shade
Crooked as channels chance hath made
It rambled as it loved to stray
And hope and feeling led the way
And birds no matter what the tune
Or croak or tweet – twas natures boon
That brought them joy – and music flung
Its spell oer every mattin sung
And een the sparrows chirp to me
Was song in its felicity
When grief hung oer me like a cloud
Till hope seemed even in her shroud
I whispered poesys spells till they
Gleamed round me like a summers day
When tempests oer my labour sung
My soul to its responses rung
And joined the chorus till the storm
Fell all unheeded void of harm

And each old leaning shielding tree
Were princely pallaces to me
Where I would sit me down and chime
My unheard rhapsodies to ryhme

* * *

– Had I but felt amid my toil
That I in days to come should be
A little light in minstrelsy
And in the blush of after days
Win beautys smile and beautys praise
My heart with lonely fancy warm
Had even bursted with the charm
And Mary thou whose very name
I loved whose look was even fame
From those delicious eyes of blue
In smiles and rapture ever new
Thy timid step thy fairy form
Thy face with blushes ever warm
When praise my schoolboy heart did move
I saw thy blush and thought it love
And all ambitious thee to please
My heart was ever ill at ease
I saw thy beauty grow with days
And tryed song pictures in thy praise
And all of fair or beautiful
Were thine akin – nor could I pull

The blossoms that I thought divine
Lest I should injure aught of thine
So where they grew I let them be
And tho' I dare not look to thee
Of love – to them I talked aloud
And grew ambitious from the crowd
With hopes that I should one day be
Beloved Mary een by thee
But I mistook in early day
The world – and so our hopes decay
Yet that same cheer in after toils
Was poesy – and still she smiles

From THE ETERNITY OF NATURE

Leaves from eternity are simple things
To the worlds gaze where to a spirit clings
Sublime and lasting – trampled underfoot
The daisey lives and strikes its little root
Into the lap of time – centurys may come
And pass away into the silent tomb
And still the child hid in the womb of time
Shall smile and pluck them when this simple
ryhme
Shall be forgotten like a church yard stone
Or lingering lye unnotised and alone
When eighteen hundred years our common date
Grows many thousands in their marching state
Aye still the child with pleasure in his eye
Shall cry the daisy a familiar cry
And run to pluck it – in the self same state
As when time found it in his infant date
And like a child himself when all was new
Wonder might smile and make him notice too

THE MORES

Far spread the moorey ground a level scene
Bespread with rush and one eternal green
That never felt the rage of blundering plough
Though centurys wreathed springs blossoms on its
  brow
Still meeting plains that stretched them far away
In uncheckt shadows of green brown and grey
Unbounded freedom ruled the wandering scene
Nor fence of ownership crept in between
To hide the prospect of the following eye
Its only bondage was the circling sky
One mighty flat undwarfed by bush and tree
Spread its faint shadow of immensity
And lost itself which seemed to eke its bounds
In the blue mist the orisons edge surrounds
Now this sweet vision of my boyish hours
Free as spring clouds and wild as summer flowers
Is faded all – a hope that blossomed free
And hath been once no more shall ever be
Inclosure came and trampled on the grave
Of labours rights and left the poor a slave
And memorys pride ere want to wealth did bow
Is both the shadow and the substance now
The sheep and cows were free to range as then
Where change might prompt nor felt the bonds of
  men

Cows went and came with evening morn and
night
To the wild pasture as their common right
And sheep unfolded with the rising sun
Heard the swains shout and felt their freedom
won
Tracked the red fallow field and heath and plain
Then met the brook and drank and roamed again
The brook that dribbled on as clear as glass
Beneath the roots they hid among the grass
While the glad shepherd traced their tracks along
Free as the lark and happy as her song
But now alls fled and flats of many a dye
That seemed to lengthen with the following eye
Moors loosing from the sight far smooth and blea
Where swopt the plover in its pleasure free
Are vanished now with commons wild and gay
As poets visions of lifes early day
Mulberry bushes where the boy would run
To fill his hands with fruit are grubbed and done
And hedgrow briars – flower lovers overjoyed
Came and got flower pots – these are all destroyed
And sky bound mores in mangled garbs are left
Like mighty giants of their limbs bereft
Fence now meets fence in owners little bounds
Of field and meadow large as garden grounds
In little parcels little minds to please
With men and flocks imprisoned ill at ease

Each little path that led its pleasant way
As sweet as morning leading night astray
Where little flowers bloomed round a varied host
That travel felt delighted to be lost
Nor grudged the steps that he had taen as vain
When right roads traced his journeys end again
Nay on a broken tree hed sit awhile
To see the mores and fields and meadows smile
Sometimes with cowslaps smothered – then all
  white
With daiseys – then the summers splendid sight
Of corn fields crimson oer the 'headach' bloomd
Like splendid armys for the battle plumed
He gazed upon them with wild fancys eye
As fallen landscapes from an evening sky
These paths are stopt – the rude philistines thrall
Is laid upon them and destroyed them all
Each little tyrant with his little sign
Shows where man claims earth glows no more
  divine
On paths to freedom and to childhood dear
A board sticks up to notice 'no road here'
And on the tree with ivy overhung
The hated sign by vulgar taste is hung
As tho the very birds should learn to know
When they go there they must no further go
This with the poor scared freedom bade good bye
And much the[y] feel it in the smothered sigh

And birds and trees and flowers without a name
All sighed when lawless laws enclosure came
And dreams of plunder in such rebel schemes
Have found too truly that they were but dreams

WINTER FIELDS

O for a pleasant book to cheat the sway
Of winter – where rich mirth with hearty laugh
Listens and rubs his legs on corner seat
For fields are mire and sludge – and badly off
Are those who on their pudgy paths delay
There striding shepherd seeking driest way
Fearing night's wetshod feet and hacking cough
That keeps him waken till the peep of day
Goes shouldering onward and with ready hook
Progs oft to ford the sloughs that nearly meet
Across the lands – croodling and thin to view
His loath dog follows – stops and quakes and
  looks
For better roads – till whistled to pursue
Then on with frequent jump he hirkles through

THE FODDERING BOY

The foddering boy along the crumping snows
With strawband-belted legs and folded arm
Hastens and on the blast that keenly blows
Oft turns for breath and beats his fingers warm
And shakes the lodging snows from off his cloaths
Buttoning his doublet closer from the storm
And slouching his brown beaver o'er his nose
Then faces it agen – and seeks the stack
Within its circling fence – where hungry lows
Expecting cattle making many a track
About the snows – impatient for the sound
When in hugh forkfulls trailing at his back
He litters the sweet hay about the ground
And brawls to call the staring cattle round

LOVE AND MEMORY

Thou art gone the dark journey
That leaves no returning
Tis fruitless to mourn thee
But who can help mourning
To think of the life
That did laugh on thy brow
In the beautiful past
Left so desolate now

When youth seemed immortal
So sweet did it weave
Heavens haloo around thee
Earths hopes to decieve
Thou fairest and dearest
Where many were fair
To my heart thou art nearest
Though this name is but there

The nearer the fountain
More pure the stream flows
And sweeter to fancy
The bud of the rose
And now thourt in heaven
More pure is the birth
Of thoughts that wake of thee
Than ought upon earth

As a bud green in spring
As a rose blown in June
Thy beauty looked out
And departed as soon
Heaven saw thee too fair
For earths tennants of clay
And ere age did thee wrong
Thou wert summoned away

I know thou art happy
Why in grief need I be
Yet I am and the more so
To feel its for thee
For thy presence possest
As thy abscence destroyed
The most that I loved
And the all I enjoyed

So I try to seek pleasure
But vainly I try
Now joys cup is drained
And hopes fountain is dry
I mix with the living
Yet what do I see
Only more cause for sorrow
In loosing of thee

The year has its winter
As well as its May
So the sweetest must leave us
And the fairest decay
Suns leave us to night
And their light none may borrow
So joy retreats from us
Overtaken by sorrow

The sun greets the spring
And the blossom the bee
The grass the blea hill
And the leaf the bare tree
But suns nor yet seasons
As sweet as they be
Shall ever more greet me
With tidings of thee

The voice of the cuckoo
Is merry at noon
And the song of the nightingale
Gladdens the moon
But the gayest to day
May be saddest to morrow
And the loudest in joy
Sink the deepest in sorrow

For the lovely in death
And the fairest must die
Fall once and for ever
Like stars from the sky
So in vain do I mourn thee
I know its in vain
Who would wish thee from joy
To earths troubles again

Yet thy love shed upon me
Life more then mine own
And now thou art from me
My being is gone
Words know not my grief
Thus without thee to dwell
Yet in one I felt all
When life bade thee farewell

SABBATH BELLS

Ive often on a sabbath day
Where pastoral quiet dwells
Lay down among the new mown hay
To listen distant bells
That beautifully flung the sound
Upon the quiet wind
While beans in blossom breathed around
A fragrance oer the mind

A fragrance and a joy beside
That never wears away
The very air seems deified
Upon a sabbath day
So beautiful the flitting wrack
Slow pausing from the eye
Earths music seemed to call them back
Calm settled in the sky

And I have listened till I felt
A feeling not in words
A love that rudest moods would melt
When those sweet sounds was heard
A melancholly joy at rest
A pleasurable pain
A love a rapture of the breast
That nothing will explain

A dream of beauty that displays
Ima[g]inary joys
That all the world in all its ways
Finds not to realize
All idly stretched upon the hay
The wind-flirt fanning bye
How soft how sweetly swept away
The music of the sky

The ear it lost and caught the sound
Swelled beautifully on
A fitful melody around
Of sweetness heard and gone
I felt such thoughts I yearned to sing
The humming airs delight
That seemed to move the swallows wing
Into a wilder flight

The butterflye in wings of brown
Would find me where I lay
Fluttering and bobbing up and down
And settling on the hay
The waving blossoms seemed to throw
Their fragrance to the sound
While up and down and loud and low
The bells were ringing round

SAND MARTIN

Thou hermit haunter of the lonely glen
And common wild and heath – the desolate face
Of rude waste landscapes far away from men
Where frequent quarrys give thee dwelling place
With strangest taste and labour undeterred
Drilling small holes along the quarrys side
More like the haunts of vermin than a bird
And seldom by the nesting boy descried
Ive seen thee far away from all thy tribe
Flirting about the unfrequented sky
And felt a feeling that I cant describe
Of lone seclusion and a hermit joy
To see thee circle round nor go beyond
That lone heath and its melancholly pond

THE NIGHTINGALES NEST

Up this green woodland ride lets softly rove
And list the nightingale – she dwelleth here
Hush let the wood gate softly clap – for fear
The noise may drive her from her home of love
For here Ive heard her many a merry year
At morn and eve nay all the live long day
As though she lived on song – this very spot
Just where that old mans beard all wildly trails
Rude arbours oer the road and stops the way
And where that child its blue bell flowers hath
  got
Laughing and creeping through the mossy rails
There have I hunted like a very boy
Creeping on hands and knees through matted
  thorns
To find her nest and see her feed her young
And vainly did I many hours employ
All seemed as hidden as a thought unborn
And where these crimping fern leaves ramp
  among
The hazels under boughs – Ive nestled down
And watched her while she sung – and her
  renown
Hath made me marvel that so famed a bird
Should have no better dress than russet brown
Her wings would tremble in her extacy

And feathers stand on end as twere with joy
And mouth wide open to release her heart
Of its out sobbing songs – the happiest part
Of summers fame she shared – for so to me
Did happy fancys shapen her employ
But if I touched a bush or scarcely stirred
All in a moment stopt – I watched in vain
The timid bird had left the hazel bush
And at a distance hid to sing again
Lost in a wilderness of listening leaves
Rich extacy would pour its luscious strain
Till envy spurred the emulating thrush
To start less wild and scarce inferior songs
For cares with him for half the year remain
To damp the ardour of his speckled breast
While nightingales to summers life belongs
And naked trees and winters nipping wrongs
Are strangers to her music and her rest
Her joys are evergreen her world is wide
– Hark there she is as usual lets be hush
For in this black thorn clump if rightly guest
Her curious house is hidden – part aside
These hazle branches in a gentle way
And stoop right cautious neath the rustling
  boughs
For we will have another search to day
And hunt this fern strown thorn clump round
  and round

And where this seeded wood grass idly bows
Well wade right through – it is a likely nook
In such like spots and often on the ground
They'll build where rude boys never think to look
Aye as I live her secret nest is here
Upon this white thorn stulp – Ive searched about
For hours in vain – there put that bramble bye
Nay trample on its branshes and get near
How subtle is the bird she started out
And raised a plaintive note of danger nigh
Ere we were past the brambles and now near
Her nest she sudden stops – as choaking fear
That might betray her home so even now
Well leave it as we found it – safetys guard
Of pathless solitude shall keep it still
See there shes sitting on the old oak bough
Mute in her fears our presence doth retard
Her joys and doubt turns all her rapture chill
Sing on sweet bird may no worse hap befall
Thy visions then the fear that now decieves
We will not plunder music of its dower
Nor turn this spot of happiness to thrall
For melody seems hid in every flower
That blossoms near thy home – these harebells all
Seems bowing with the beautiful in song
And gaping cuckoo with its spotted leaves
Seems blushing of the singing it has heard
How curious is the nest no other bird
Uses such loose materials or weaves

Their dwellings in such spots – dead oaken leaves
Are placed without and velvet moss within
And little scraps of grass – and scant and spare
Of what seems scarce materials down and hair
For from mans haunts she seemeth nought to win
Yet nature is the builder and contrives
Homes for her childerns comfort even here
Where solitudes deciples spend their lives
Unseen save when a wanderer passes near
That loves such pleasant places – deep adown
The nest is made an hermits mossy cell
Snug lie her curious eggs in number five
Of deadend green or rather olive brown
And the old prickly thorn bush guards them well
And here well leave them still unknown to wrong
As the old woodlands legacy of song

THE FIRETAILS NEST

Tweet pipes the robin as the cat creeps bye
Her nestling young that in the elderns lie
And then the bluecap tootles in its glee
Picking the flies from blossomed apple tree
And pink the chaffinch cries its well known strain
Urging its mate to utter pink again
While in a quiet mood hedgsparrows trie
An inward stir of shadowed melody
While on the rotten tree the firetail mourns
As the old hedger to his toil returns
And chops the grain to stop the gap close bye
The hole where her blue eggs in safety lie
Of every thing that stirs she dreameth wrong
And pipes her 'tweet tut' fears the whole day long

THE AUTUMN ROBIN

Sweet little Bird in russet coat
  The livery of the closing year
I love thy lonely plaintive note
  And tiney whispering song to hear
While on the stile or garden seat
  I sit to watch the falling leaves
Thy songs thy little joys repeat
  My lonliness relieves

And many are the lonely minds
  That hear and welcome thee anew
Not taste alone but humble hinds
  Delight to praise and love thee too
The veriest clown beside his cart
  Turns from his song with many a smile
To see thee from the hedgrow start
  And sing upon the stile

The Shepherd on the fallen tree
  Drops down to listen to thy lay
And chides his dog beside his knee
  Who barks and frightens thee away
The hedger pauses ere he knocks
  The stake down in the meadow gap
– The Boy who every songster mocks
  Forbears the gate to clap

When in the hedge that hides the post
  Thy ruddy bosom he surveys
Pleased with thy song in pleasure lost
  He pausing mutters scraps of praise
The maiden marks at days decline
  Thee in the yard on broken plough
And stops her song to listen thine
  While milking brindled cow

Thy simple faith in mans esteem
  From every heart that favours won
Dangers to thee no dangers seem
  Thou seemest to court them more then shun
The clown in winter takes his gun
  The barn door flocking birds to slay
Yet shouldst thou in the danger run
  He turns the tube away

The gipsey boy who seeks in glee
  Blackberrys for a dainty meal
Laughs loud on first beholding thee
  When called so near his presence steal
For sure he thinks thou knew the call
  And tho his hunger ill can spare
The fruit he will not pluck them all
  But leaves some to thy share

Up on the ditchers spade thoult hop
  For grubs and wreathing worms to search
Where woodmen in the Forrests chop
  Thoult fearless on their faggots perch
Nay by the gipseys camp I stop
  And mark thee perch a moment there
To prune thy wing awhile then drop
  The littered crumbs to share

Domestic bird thy pleasant face
  Doth well thy common suit commend
To meet thee in a stranger place
  Is meeting with an ancient friend
I track the thickets glooms around
  And there as loath to leave agen
Thou comest as if thou knew the sound
  And loved the sight of men

The lonliest wood that man can trace
  To thee a pleasant dwelling gives
In every town and crowded place
  The sweet domestic Robin lives
Go where we will in every spot
  Thy little welcome mates appear
And like the daiseys common lot
  Thourt met with every where

The swallow in the chimney tier
    The tittering martin in the eaves
With half of love and half of fear
  Their mortared dwelling shyly weaves
The sparrows in the thatch will shield
  Yet they as well as eer they can
Contrive with doubtful faith to build
  Beyond the reach of man

But thourt less timid then the Wren
  Domestic and confiding bird
And spots the nearest haunts of men
  Are oftenest for thy home prefered
In garden walls thoult build so low
  Close where the bunch of fennel stands
That een a child just learned to go
  May reach with tiny hands

Sweet favoured bird thy under notes
  In summers music grows unknown
The conscert from a thousand throats
  Leaves thee as if to pipe alone
No listening ear the shepherd lends
  The simple ploughman marks thee not
And then by all thy autumn friends
  Thourt missing and forgot

The far famed nightingale that shares
   Cold public praise from every tongue
The popular voice of music heirs
   And injures much thy under song
Yet then my walks thy theme salutes
   And finds their autumn favoured guest
Gay piping on the hazel roots
   Above thy mossy nest

Tis wrong that thou shouldst be despised
   When these gay fickle birds appear
They sing when summer flowers are prized
   Thou at the dull and dying year
Well let the heedless and the gay
   Bepraise the voice of louder lays
The joy thou stealst from sorrows day
   Is more to thee then praise

And could my notes steal aught from thine
   My words but immitate thy lay
Time would not then his charge resign
   Nor throw the meanest verse away
But ever at this mellow time
   He should thine Autumn praise prolong
So would they share eternal prime
   With daiseys and thy song

THE BLACKCAP

Under the twigs the blackcap hangs in vain
With snowwhite patch streaked over either eye
This way and that he turns and peeps again
As wont where silk-cased insects used to lie
But summer leaves are gone the day is bye
For happy holidays and now he fares
But cloudy like the weather yet to view
He flirts a happy wing and inly wears
Content in gleaning what the orchard spares
And like his little couzin capped in blue
Domesticates the lonely winter through
In homestead plots and gardens where he wears
Familiar pertness – yet but seldom comes
With the tame robin to the door for crumbs

TO THE SNIPE

Lover of swamps
The quagmire overgrown
With hassock tufts of sedge – where fear
  encamps
Around thy home alone

The trembling grass
Quakes from the human foot
Nor bears the weight of man to let him pass
Where he alone and mute

Sitteth at rest
In safety neath the clump
Of hugh flag-forrest that thy haunts invest
Or some old sallow stump

Thriving on seams
That tiney islands swell
Just hilling from the mud and rancid streams
Suiting thy nature well

For here thy bill
Suited by wisdom good
Of rude unseemly length doth delve and drill
The gelid mass for food

And here may hap
When summer suns hath drest
The moors rude desolate and spungy lap
May hide thy mystic nest

Mystic indeed
For isles that ocean make
Are scarcely more secure for birds to build
Then this flag-hidden lake

Boys thread the woods
To their remotest shades
But in these marshy flats these stagnant floods
Security pervades

From year to year
Places untrodden lye
Where man nor boy nor stock hath ventured
near
– Nought gazed on but the sky

And fowl that dread
The very breath of man
Hiding in spots that never knew his tread
A wild and timid clan

Wigeon and teal
And wild duck – restless lot
That from mans dreaded sight will ever steal
To the most dreary spot

Here tempests howl
Around each flaggy plot
Where they who dread mans sight the water
  fowl
Hide and are frighted not

Tis power divine
That heartens them to brave
The roughest tempest and at ease recline
On marshes or the wave

Yet instinct knows
Not safetys bounds to shun
The firmer ground where skulking fowler goes
With searching dogs and gun

By tepid springs
Scarcely one stride across
Though brambles from its edge a shelter flings
Thy safety is at loss

And never chuse
The little sinky foss
Streaking the moores whence spa-red water
spews
From puddles fringed with moss

Free booters there
Intent to kill and slay
Startle with cracking guns the trepid air
And dogs thy haunts betray

From dangers reach
Here thou art safe to roam
Far as these washy flag-worn marshes stretch
A still and quiet home

In these thy haunts
Ive gleaned habitual love
From the vague world where pride and folly
taunts
I muse and look above

Thy solitudes
The unbounded heaven esteems
And here my heart warms into higher moods
And dignifying dreams

I see the sky
Smile on the meanest spot
Giving to all that creep or walk or flye
A calm and cordial lot

Thine teaches me
Right feelings to employ
That in the dreariest places peace will be
A dweller and a joy

REMEMBRANCES

Summer pleasures they are gone like to visions every one
And the cloudy days of autumn and of winter cometh
  on
I tried to call them back but unbidden they are gone
Far away from heart and eye and for ever far away
Dear heart and can it be that such raptures meet
  decay
I thought them all eternal when by Langley bush I lay
I thought them joys eternal when I used to shout and
  play
On its bank at 'clink and bandy' 'chock' and 'taw' and
  ducking stone
Where silence sitteth now on the wild heath as her own
Like a ruin of the past all alone

When I used to lie and sing by old eastwells boiling
  spring
When I used to tie the willow boughs together for a
  'swing'
And fish with crooked pins and thread and never
  catch a thing
With heart just like a feather – now as heavy as a
  stone
When beneath old lea close oak I the bottom branches
  broke
To make our harvest cart like so many working folk
And then to cut a straw at the brook to have a soak

O I never dreamed of parting or that trouble had a
sting
Or that pleasures like a flock of birds would ever take
to wing
Leaving nothing but a little naked spring

When jumping time away on old cross berry way
And eating awes like sugar plumbs ere they had lost
the may
And skipping like a leveret before the peep of day
On the rolly polly up and downs of pleasant swordy
well
When in round oaks narrow lane as the south got
black again
We sought the hollow ash that was shelter from the
rain
With our pockets full of peas we had stolen from the
grain
How delicious was the dinner time on such a showry
day
O words are poor receipts for what time hath stole away
The ancient pulpit trees and the play

When for school oer 'little field' with its brook and
wooden brig
Where I swaggered like a man though I was not half so
big
While I held my little plough though twas but a willow
twig

And drove my team along made of nothing but a
name
'Gee hep' and 'hoit' and 'woi' – O I never call to mind
These pleasant names of places but I leave a sigh
behind
While I see the little mouldywharps hang sweeing to
the wind
On the only aged willow that in all the field remains
And nature hides her face where theyre sweeing in
their chains
And in a silent murmuring complains

Here was commons for their hills where they seek for
freedom still
Though every commons gone and though traps are set
to kill
The little homeless miners – O it turns my bosom chill
When I think of old 'sneap green' puddocks nook and
hilly snow
Where bramble bushes grew and the daisy gemmed in
dew
And the hills of silken grass like to cushions to the view
Where we threw the pissmire crumbs when we'd
nothing else to do
All leveled like a desert by the never weary plough
All vanished like the sun where that cloud is passing
now
All settled here for ever on its brow

O I never thought that joys would run away from boys
Or that boys would change their minds and forsake
such summer joys
But alack I never dreamed that the world had other toys
To petrify first feelings like the fable into stone
Till I found the pleasure past and a winter come at last
Then the fields were sudden bare and the sky got
overcast
And boyhoods pleasing haunts like a blossom in the
blast
Was shrivelled to a withered weed and trampled down
and done
Till vanished was the morning spring and set that
summer sun
And winter fought her battle strife and won

By Langley bush I roam but the bush hath left its hill
On cowper green I stray tis a desert strange and chill
And spreading lea close oak ere decay had penned its
will
To the axe of the spoiler and self interest fell a prey
And cross berry way and old round oaks narrow lane
With its hollow trees like pulpits I shall never see again
Inclosure like a Buonaparte let not a thing remain
It levelled every bush and tree and levelled every hill
And hung the moles for traitors – though the brook is
running still
It runs a naked brook cold and chill

O had I known as then joy had left the paths of men
I had watched her night and day besure and never
slept agen
And when she turned to go O I'd caught her mantle
then
And wooed her like a lover by my lonely side to stay
Aye knelt and worshiped on as love in beautys bower
And clung upon her smiles as a bee upon a flower
And gave her heart my poesys all cropt in a sunny
hour
As keepsakes and pledges all to never fade away
But love never heeded to treasure up the may
So it went the common road with decay

From CHILD HAROLD

Introduction

Many are poets – though they use no pen
To show their labours to the shuffling age
Real poets must be truly honest men
Tied to no mongrel laws on flatterys page
No zeal have they for wrong or party rage
– The life of labour is a rural song
That hurts no cause – nor warfare tries to wage
Toil like the brook in music wears along –
Great little minds claim right to act the wrong

BALLAD

Sweet days while God your blessings send
I call your joys my own
– And if I have an only friend
I am not left alone

She sees the fields the trees the spires
Which I can daily see
And if true love her heart inspires
Life still has joys for me

She sees the wild flower in the dells
That in my rambles shine
The sky that oer her homstead dwells
Looks sunny over mine

The cloud that passes where she dwells
In less then half an hour
Darkens around these orchard dells
Or melts a sudden shower

The wind that leaves the sunny south
And fans the orchard tree
Might steal the kisses from her mouth
And waft her voice to me

O when will autumn bring the news
Now harvest browns the fen
That Mary as my vagrant muse
And I shall meet again

SONG

The spring may forget that he reigns in the sky
And winter again hide her flowers in the snow
The summer may thirst when her fountains are dry
But I'll think of Mary wherever I go
The bird may forget that her nest is begun
When the snow settles white on the new budding tree
And nature in tempests forget the bright sun
But I'll ne'er forget her – that was plighted to me

How could I – how should I – that loved her so early
Forget – when I've sung of her beauty in song
How could I forget – what I've worshiped so dearly
From boyhood to manhood – and all my life long –
How could I forget – what I've worshipped to dearly
From boyhood to manhood – and all my life long –
As leaves to the branches in summer comes duly
And blossoms will bloom on the stalk and the tree
To her beauty I'll cling – and I'll love her as truly
And think of sweet Mary wherever I be

SONG

Tis autumn now and natures scenes
The pleachy fields and yellowing trees
Looses their blooming hues and greens
But nature finds no change in me
The fading woods the russet grange
The hues of nature may desert
But nought in me shall find a change
To wrong the angel of my heart
For Mary is my angel still
Through every month and every ill

The leaves they loosen from the branch
And fall upon the gusty wind
But my hearts silent love is staunch
And nought can tear her from my mind
The flowers are gone from dell and bower
Though crowds from summers lap was
  given
But love is an eternal flower
Like purple amaranths in heaven
To Mary first my heart did bow
And if she's true she keeps it now

Just as the summer keeps the flower
Which spring consceaèled in hoods of gold
Or unripe harvest met the shower
And made earths blessings manifold
Just so my Mary lives for me
A silent thought for months and years
The world may live in revellry
Her name my lonely quiet cheers
And cheer it will what e'er may be
While Mary lives to think of me

SONG

The floods come oer the meadow leas
The dykes are full and brimming
Field furrows reach the horses knees
Where wild ducks oft are swimming
The skyes are black the fields are bare
The trees their coats are loosing
The leaves are dancing in the air
The sun its warmth refusing

Brown are the flags and fadeing sedge
And tanned the meadow plains
Bright yellow is the osier hedge
Beside the brimming drains
The crows sit on the willow tree
The lake is full below
But still the dullest thing I see
Is self that wanders slow

The dullest scenes are not so dull
As thoughts I cannot tell
The brimming dykes are not so full
As my hearts silent swell
I leave my troubles to the winds
With none to share a part
The only joy my feeling finds
Hides in an aching heart

4

Now Come The Balm And Breezes Of The Spring
Not With The Pleasure's Of My Early Day's
When Nature Seemed One Endless Song To Sing
A Joyous Melody And Happy Praise
Ah Would They Come Agen – But Life Betrays
Quicksands And Gulphs And Storms That Howl
And Sting
All Quiet Into Madness And Delays
Care Hides The Sunshine With Its Raven Wing
And Hell Glooms Sadness Oer The Songs of
Spring

5

Like Satans Warcry First In Paradise
When Love Lay Sleeping On The Flowery Slope
Like Virtue Wakeing In The Arms Of Vice
Or Deaths Sea Bursting In The Midst Of Hope
Sorrows Will Stay – And Pleasures Will Elope
In The Uncertain Cartnty Of Care
Joys Bounds Are Narrow But A Wider Scope
Is Left For Trouble Which Our Life Must Bear
Of Which All Human Life Is More Or Less The
Heir

7

What Is The Orphan Child without A Friend
That Knows No Fathers Care Or Mothers Love
No Leading Hand His Infant Steps Defend
And None To Notice But His God Above
No Joy's Are Seen His Little Heart To Move
Care Turns All Joys to Dross And Nought To
Gold
And Smiles In Fancys Time May Still Disprove
Growing To Cares And Sorrow's Menifold
Bird Of The Waste A Lamb Without A Fold

8

No Mothers Love or Fathers Care Have They
Left To The Storms Of Fate Like Creatures Wild
They Live Like Blossoms In The Winters Day
E'en Nature Frowns Upon The Orphan Child
On Whose Young Face A Mother Never Smiled
Foolhardy Care Increasing With His Years
From Friends And Joys Of Every Kind Exiled
Even Old In Care The Infant Babe Appears
And Many A Mother Meets Its Face in Tears

10

But Providence That Grand Eternal Calm
Is With Him Like The Sunshine In The Sky
Nature Our Kindest Mother Void of Harm
Watches The Orphan's Lonely Infancy
Strengthening The Man When Childhoods Cares
Are Bye
She Nurses Still Young Unreproached Distress
And Hears The Lonely Infants Every Sigh
Who Finds At Length To Make Its Sorrows Less
Mid Earths Cold Curses There Is One To Bless

11

Sweet Rural Maids Made Beautifull By Health
Brought Up Where Natures Calm Encircles All
Where Simple Love Remains As Sterling Wealth
Where Simple Habits Early Joys Recall
Of Youthfull Feelings Which No Wiles Enthrall
The Happy Milk Maid In Her Mean Array
Fresh As The New Blown Rose Outblooms Them
All
E'en Queens Might Sigh To Be As Blest As They
While Milkmaids Laugh And Sing Their Cares
Away

12

How Doth Those Scenes Which Rural Mirth
  Endears
Revise Old Feelings That My Youth Hath Known
And Paint The Faded Bloom Of Earlier Years
And Soften Feelings Petrefied To Stone
Joy Fled And Care Proclaimed Itself My Own
Farewells I Took Of Joys In Earliest Years
And Found The Greatest Bliss To Be Alone
My Manhood Was Eclipsed But Not In Fears
– Hell Came In Curses And She Laughd At Tears

13

But Memory Left Sweet Traces Of Her Smiles
Which I Remember Still And Still Endure
The Shadows Of First Loves My Heart Beguiles
Time Brought Both Pain And Pleasure But No
  Cure
Sweet Bessey Maid Of Health And Fancys Pure
How Did I Woo Thee Once – Still Unforgot
But Promises In Love Are Never Sure
And Where We Met How Dear Is Every Spot
And Though We Parted Still I Murmur Not

14

For Loves However Dear Must Meet With Clouds
And Ties Made Tight Get Loose And May Be
Parted
Springs First Young Flowers The Winter Often
Shrouds
And Loves First Hopes Are Very Often Thwarted
E'en Mine Beat High And Then Fell Broken
Hearted
And Sorrow Mourned In Verse To Reconscile
My Feelings To My Fate Though Lone And Parted
Loves Enemies Are Like The Scorpion Vile
That Oer Its Ruined Hopes Will Hiss And Smile

15

Yet Love Lives On In Every Kind of Weather
In Heat And Cold In Sunshine And In Gloom
Winter May Blight And Stormy Clouds May
Gather
Nature Invigorates And Love Will Bloom
It Fears No Sorrow In A Life To Come
But Lives Within Itself From Year To Year
As Doth The Wild Flower In Its Own Perfume
As In The Lapland Snows Springs Blooms Appear
So True Love Blooms And Blossoms Every Where

19

The Dew falls on the weed and on the flower
The rose and thistle bathe their heads in dew
The lowliest heart may have its prospering hour
The sadest bosom meet its wishes true
E'en I may joy love happiness renew
Though not the sweets of my first early days
When one sweet face was all the loves I knew
And my soul trembled on her eyes to gaze
Whose very censure seemed intended praise

20

A soul within the heart that loves the more
Giving to pains and fears eternal life
Burning the flesh till it consumes the core
So Love is still the eternal calm of strife
Thou soul within a soul thou life of life
Thou Essence of my hopes and fears and joys
M—y my dear first love and early wife
And still the flower my inmost soul enjoys
Thy love's the bloom no canker worm destroys

21

Flow on my verse though barren thou mayest be
Of thought – Yet sing and let thy fancys roll
In Early days thou sweept a mighty sea
All calm in troublous deeps and spurned controul
Thou fire and iceberg to an aching soul
And still an angel in my gloomy way
Far better opiate then the draining bowl
Still sing my muse to drive cares fiends away
Nor heed what loitering listener hears the lay

22

My themes be artless cots and happy plains
Though far from man my wayward fancies flee
Of fields and woods rehearse in willing strains
And I mayhap may feed on joys with thee
These cowslip fields this sward my pillow be
So I may sleep the sun into the west
My cot this awthorn hedge this spreading tree
– Mary and Martha once my daily guests
And still as mine both wedded loved and blest

23

I rest my wearied life in these sweet fields
Reflecting every smile in natures face
And much of joy this grass – These hedges yields
Not found in citys where crowds daily trace
Heart pleasures there hath no abideing place
The star gemmed early morn the silent even
Hath pleasures that our broken hopes deface
To love too well leaves nought to be forgiven
The Gates of Eden is the bounds of heaven

24

The apathy that fickle love wears through
The doubts and certaintys are still akin
Its every joy has sorrow in the view
Its holy truth like Eve's beguileing sin
Seems to be losses even while we win
Tormenting joys and cheating into wrong
And still we love – and fall into the Gin
My sun of love was short – and clouded long
And now its shadow fills a feeble song

'LORD HEAR MY PRAYER WHEN TROUBLE GLOOMS'

Lord hear my prayer when trouble glooms
Let sorrow find a way
And when the day of trouble comes
Turn not thy face away
My bones like hearth stones burn away
My life like vapoury smoke decays

My heart is smitten like the grass
That withered lies and dead
And I so lost to what I was
Forget to eat my bread
My voice is groaning all the day
My bones prick through this skin of clay

The wildernesses pelican
The deserts lonely owl
I am their like a desert man
In ways as lone and foul
As sparrows on the cottage top
I wait till I with faintness drop

I bear my enemies reproach
All silently I mourn
They on my private peace encroach
Against me they are sworn
Ashes as bread my trouble shares
And mix my food with weeping cares

Yet not for them is sorrows toil
I fear no mortals frown
But thou hast held me up awhile
And thou hast cast me down
My days like shadows waste from view
I mourn like withered grass in dew

But thou Lord shalt endure forever
All generations through
Thou shalt to Zion be the giver
Of joy and mercey too
Her very stones are in their trust
Thy servants reverence her dust

Heathens shall hear and fear thy name
All kings of earth thy glory know
When thou shalt build up Zions fame
And live in glory there below
He'll not despise their prayers though mute
But still regard the destitute

SONG LAST DAY

There is a day a dreadfull day
Still following the past
When sun and moon are past away
And mingle with the blast
There is a vision in my eye
A vacuum oer my mind
Sometimes as on the sea I lye
Mid roaring waves and wind

When valleys rise to mountain waves
And mountains sink to seas
When towns and cities temples graves
All vanish like a breeze
The skyes that was are past and oer
That almanack of days
Year chronicles are kept no more
Oblivions ruin pays

Pays in destruction shades and hell
Sin goes in darkness down
And therein sulphurs shadows dwell
Worths wins and wears the crown
The very shore if shore I see
All shrivelled to a scroll
The Heaven's rend away from me
And thunders sulphurs roll

Black as the deadly thunder cloud
The stars shall turn to dun
And heaven by that darkness bowed
Shall make days light be done
When stars and skys shall all decay
And earth no more shall be
When heaven itself shall pass away
Then thou'lt remember me

'THE THUNDER MUTTERS LOUDER AND MORE LOUD'

The thunder mutters louder and more loud
With quicker motion hay folks ply the rake
Ready to burst slow sails the pitch black cloud
And all the gang a bigger haycock make
To sit beneath – the woodland winds awake
The drops so large wet all thro' in an hour
A tiney flood runs down the leaning rake
In the sweet hay yet dry the hay folks cower
And some beneath the waggon shun the shower

MARY

1

It is the evening hour,
How silent all doth lie,
The horned moon she shews her face,
In the river, with the sky;
Just by the path on which we pass,
The flaggy lake, lies still, as glass.

2

Spirit of her I love,
Wispering to me:
Stories of sweet visions, as I rove:
Here stop and crop with me,
Sweet flowers, that in the still hour grew,
We'll take them home, nor shake off the
bright dew.

3

Mary, or sweet spirit of thee,
As the bright sun shines tomorrow;
Thy dark eyes these flowers shall see,
Gathered by me in sorrow,
In the still hour, when my mind was free,
To walk alone – yet wish I walk'd with thee.

SPRING

Pale sun beams gleam
That nurtur a few flowers
Pile wort and daisey and a sprig o' green
On white thorn bushes
In the leaf strewn hedge

These harbingers
Tell spring is coming fast
And these the schoolboy marks
And wastes an hour from school
Agen the old pasture hedge

Cropping the daisey
And the pile wort flowers
Pleased with the Spring and all he looks
  upon
He opes his spelling book
And hides her blossoms there

Shadows fall dark
Like black in the pale Sun
And lye the bleak day long
Like black stock under hedges
And bare wind rocked trees

Tis chill but pleasant
In the hedge bottom lined
With brown seer leaves the last
Year littered there and left
Mopes the hedge Sparrow

With trembling wings and cheeps
Its welcome to pale sunbeams
Creeping through and further on
Made of green moss
The nest and green blue eggs are seen

All token spring and every day
Green and more green hedges and close
And every where appears
Still tis but March
But still that March is Spring

SONNET

Enough of misery keeps my heart alive
To make it feel more mental agony
Till even life itself becomes all pain
And bondage more than hell to keep alive
And still I live, nor murmer nor complain
Save that the bonds which hold me may make
  free
My lonely solitude, and give me rest
When every foe hath ceased to trouble me
On the soft throbbings of a womans breast
Where love and truth and feeling live confest
The little cottage with those bonds of joy
My family – lifes blood within my brest
Is not more dear – than is each girl and boy
Which times mature and nothing can destroy.

A LAMENT

1

The sun looks from a cloudy sky,
  On yellow bleaching reeds. –
The river streams run muddy by,
  Among the flags and reeds.
And nature seems so lost and coy,
  All silent and alone;
Left here without a single joy,
  Or love to call my own.

2

How mournful now the river seems,
  Adown the vale to run;
That ran so sweet in my young dreams,
  And glittered in the sun.
Now cold and dead, the meadow lies,
  And muddy runs the stream:
The lark on drooping pinion flies, –
  And spoiled is pleasures dream.

3

The wind comes moaning through the
  trees, –
  No maiden passes by.
And all the summer melodies, –
  Are uttered in a sigh.
On many a knoll I set me down,
  Beneath a silent sky,
And of the past all seem to frown,
  And pass in sorrow by.

AN INVITE TO ETERNITY

1

Wilt thou go with me sweet maid
Say maiden wilt thou go with me
Through the valley depths of shade
Of night and dark obscurity
Where the path hath lost its way
Where the sun forgets the day
Where there's nor life nor light to see
Sweet maiden wilt thou go with me

2

Where stones will turn to flooding streams
Where plains will rise like ocean waves
Where life will fade like visioned dreams
And mountains darken into caves
Say maiden wilt thou go with me
Through this sad non-identity
Where parents live and are forgot
And sisters live and know us not

3

Say maiden wilt thou go with me
In this strange death of life to be
To live in death and be the same
Without this life, or home, or name
At once to be, and not to be
That was, and is not – yet to see
Things pass like shadows – and the sky
Above, below, around us lie

The land of shadows wilt thou trace
And look – nor know each others face
The present mixed with reasons gone
And past, and present all as one
Say maiden can thy life be led
To join the living with the dead
Then trace thy footsteps on with me
We're wed to one eternity

'I AM'

1

I am – yet what I am, none cares or knows;
  My friends forsake me like a memory lost: –
I am the self-consumer of my woes; –
  They rise and vanish in oblivion's host,
Like shadows in love's frenzied stifled throes: –
And yet I am, and live – like vapours tost

2

Into the nothingness of scorn and noise, –
  Into the living sea of waking dreams,
Where there is neither sense of life or joys,
  But the vast shipwreck of my lifes esteems;
Even the dearest, that I love the best
Are strange – nay, rather stranger than the rest.

3

I long for scenes, where man hath never trod
  A place where woman never smiled or wept
There to abide with my Creator, God;
  And sleep as I in childhood, sweetly slept,
Untroubling, and untroubled where I lie,
The grass below – above the vaulted sky.

SONG

Love lives beyond
The tomb – the earth – which fades like dew
I love the fond
The faithfull and the true

Love lives in sleep
The happiness of healthy dreams
Eve's dews may weep
But love delightfull seems

Tis seen in flowers
And in the evens pearly dew
On earths green hours
And in the heavens eternal blue

Tis heard in spring
When light and sunbeams warm and kind
On angels wing
Bring love and music to the mind

And where is voice
So young and beautifully sweet
As natures choice
When spring and lovers meet

Love lives beyond
The tomb the earth the flowers and dew
I love the fond
The faithfull young and true

SLEEP OF SPRING

O for that sweet untroubled rest
That Poets oft have sung
The babe upon its Mothers breast
The bird upon its young
The heart asleep without a pain
When shall I know that sleep again

When shall I be as I have been
Upon my Mothers breast
Sweet nature's garb of verdant green
To woo my former rest
Lone in the meadow field and plain
And in my native wilds again

The sheep within the fallow field
The bird upon the green
The Larks that in the thistle's shield
And pipe from morn to e'en
O for the pasture fields and fen
When shall I see such rest agen

I love the weeds along the fen
More sweet then garden flowers
Freedom haunts the humble glen
That blest my happiest hours
Here prisons injure health and me
I love sweet freedom and the free

The crows upon the swelling hills
The cows upon the lea
Sheep feeding by the pasture rills
Are ever dear to me
Because sweet freedom is their mate
While I am lone and desolate

I loved the winds when I was young
When life was dear to me
I loved the song which nature sung
Endearing Liberty
I loved the wood the dale the stream
For then my boyhood used to dream

Then toil itself was even play
'Twas pleasure e'en to weep
'Twas joy to think of dreams by day
The beautifull of sleep
When shall I see the wood and plain
And dream those happy dreams again

MY EARLY HOME WAS THIS

1

Here sparrows built upon the trees
  And stock-doves hide their nest
The leaves where winnowed by the breeze
  Into a calmer rest
The black-caps song was very sweet
  That used the rose to kiss
It made the paradise complete
  My early home was this

2

The red breast from the sweet briar bush
  Drop't down to pick the worm
On the horse chesnut sang the thrush
  O'er the home where I was born
The dew morn like a shower of pearls
  Fell o'er this 'bower of bliss'
And on the bench sat boys and girls
  – My early home was this

3

The old house stooped just like a cave
  Thatched o'er with mosses green
Winter around the walls would rave
  But all was calm within
The trees they were as green agen
  Where bees the flowers would kiss
But flowers and trees seemed sweeter then
  – My early home was this –

HESPERUS

Hesperus the day is gone
Soft falls the silent dew
A tear is now on many a flower
And heaven lives in you

Hesperus the evening mild
Falls round us soft and sweet
'Tis like the breathings of a child
When day and evening meet

Hesperus the closing flower
Sleeps on the dewy ground
While dews fall in a silent shower
And heaven breathes around

Hesperus thy twinkling ray
Beams in the blue of heaven
And tells the traveller on his way
That earth shall be forgiven

SONG

1

I fly from all I prize the most
I shun what I loved best to see
My joy seems gone – my peace seems lost
And all I loved is hate to me
I shun green fields and hate the light
The glorious sun the peaceful moon
More welcome is the darkest night
Then glaring daylight comes to[o] soon

2

'Tis not the kiss that pouts to leave
The lips of woman that we love
'Tis not the world – that will deceive
Or any doubt of that above
'Tis something that my heart hath been
'Tis something that my heart approvd
'Tis something that my eyes have seen
And felt they loved –

3

I grieve not those I loved are gone
That happy years have pass'd away
That time to day keeps stealing on
To that ye call eternity
I grieve not that the seasons fade
That winter chills the summer dew
While mortal things are heavenly made
And all now doubt will soon be true

4

To thee my love, and only thee
The spring and summer seemeth true
Thy looks are like the flowers I see
Thy eyes like air-bells filled with dew
Thy look is that of happiest love
And playful as the summer sea
Thy health is from the skies above
And heaven itself is full of thee –

LOVES STORY

I do not love thee
So I'll not deceive thee
I do not love thee
Yet I'm lothe to leave thee

I do not love thee
Yet joys very essence
Comes with thy footstep
Is complete in thy presence

I do not love thee
Yet when gone I sigh
And think about thee
'Till the stars all die

I do not love thee
Yet thy black bright eyes
Bring to my hearts soul
Heaven and paradise

I do not love thee
Yet thy handsome ways
Bring me in absence
Almost hopeless days

I cannot hate thee
Yet my love seems debtor
To love thee more
So hating, love thee better

'O COULD I BE AS I HAVE BEEN'

1

O could I be as I have been
  And ne'er can be no more
A harmless thing in meadows green
  Or on the wild sea shore

2

O could I be what once I was
  In heaths and valleys green
A dweller in the summer grass
  Green fields and places green

3

A tennant of the happy fields
  By grounds of wheat and beans
By gipsey's camps and milking bield
  Where lussious woodbine leans

4

To sit on the deserted plough
  Left when the corn was sown
In corn and wild weeds buried now
  In quiet peace unknown

5

The harrows resting by the hedge
  The roll within the Dyke
Hid in the Ariff and the sedge
  Are things I used to like

6

I used to tread through fallow lands
  And wade through paths of grain
When wheat ears pattered on the hands
  And head-aches left a stain

7

I wish I was what I have been
  And what I was could be
As when I roved in shadows green
  And loved my willow tree

8

To gaze upon the starry sky
  And higher fancies build
And make in solitary joy
  Loves temple in the field

SONG

I hid my love when young while I
Coud'nt bear the buzzing of a flye
I hid my love to my despite
Till I could not bear to look at light
I dare not gaze upon her face
But left her memory in each place
Where ere I saw a wild flower lye
I kissed and bade my love good bye

I met her in the greenest dells
Where dew drops pearl the wood blue bells
The lost breeze kissed her bright blue eye
The Bee kissed and went singing bye
A sun beam found a passage there
A gold chain round her neck so fair
As secret as the wild bees song
She lay there all the summer long

I hid my love in field and town
Till e'en the breeze would knock me down
The Bees seemed singing ballads oe'r
The flyes buzz turned a Lions roar
And even silence found a tongue
To haunt me all the summer long
The Riddle nature could not prove
Was nothing else but secret love

SONG

I peeled bits o straws and I got switches too
From the grey peeling Willow as Idlers do
And I switched at the flyes as I sat all alone
Till my flesh blood and marrow wasted to dry
  bone
My illness was love though I knew not the smart
But the beauty o love was the blood o my heart

Crowded places I shunned them as noises to[o]
  rude
And flew to the silence of sweet solitude
Where the flower in green darkness, buds,
  blossoms and fades
Unseen of a shepherds and flower loving maids
The hermit bees find them but once and away
There I'll burry alive and in silence decay

I looked on the eyes o' fair woman too long
Till silence and shame stole the use o' my tongue
When I tried to speak to her I'd nothing to say
So I turned myself round and she wandered away
When she got too far off – why I'd something to
  tell
So I sent sighs behind her and talked to my sell

Willow switches I broke, and I peeled bits o
straws
Ever lonely in crowds in natures own laws
My ball room the pasture my music the Bees
My drink was the fountain my church the tall
trees
Whoever would love or be tied to a wife
When it makes a man mad a' the days o' his life

MEET ME IN THE GREEN GLEN

Love meet me in the green glen
  Beside the tall Elm tree
Where the Sweet briar smells so sweet agen
  There come wi me
    Meet me in the green glen

Meet me at the sunset
  Down in the green glen
Where we've often met
  By hawthorn tree and foxes den
    Meet me in the green glen

Meet me by the sheep pen
  Where briers smell at een
Meet me i the green glen
  Where white thorn shades are green
    Meet me in the green glen

Meet me in the green glen
  By sweet briar bushes there
Meet me by your own sen
  Where the wild thyme blossoms fair
    Meet me in the green glen

Meet me by the sweet briar
By the mole hill swelling there
When the west glows like a fire
Gods crimson bed is there
Meet me in the green glen

TO JOHN CLARE

Well honest John how fare you now at home
The spring is come and birds are building nests
The old cock robin to the stye is come
With olive feathers and its ruddy breast
And the old cock with wattles and red comb
Struts with the hens and seems to like some best
Then crows and looks about for little crumbs
Swept out bye little folks an hour ago
The pigs sleep in the sty the bookman comes
The little boys lets home close nesting go
And pockets tops and tawes where daiseys bloom
To look at the new number just laid down
With lots of pictures and good stories too
And Jack the jiant killers high renown